SAUDI ARABIA

Cath Senker

Photographs by Howard Davies

CHERRYTREE BOOKS

Titles in this series

AUSTRALIA · BANGLADESH · BRAZIL · CANADA · CHINA COSTA RICA · EGYPT · FRANCE · GERMANY · GREECE INDIA · INDONESIA · ITALY · JAMAICA · JAPAN · KENYA MEXICO · NIGERIA · PAKISTAN · RUSSIA · SAUDI ARABIA SOUTH AFRICA · SPAIN · SWEDEN · THE USA

A Cherrytree Book

Conceived and produced by

Nutshell
MEDIA

www.nutshellmedialtd.co.uk

First published in 2007 by
Evans Brothers Ltd
2A Portman Mansions
Chiltern Street
London W1U 6NR

Editor: Polly Goodman
Designer: Tim Mayer
Map artwork: Encompass Graphics Ltd
All other artwork: Tim Mayer
All photographs were taken by Howard Davies, except p14
(top): courtesy of the Royal Embassy of Saudi Arabia.

Acknowledgements
The photographer would like to thank Abdulatef and his
family and friends, Haitham Mahmoud Rushdi, Tharal and
Amira Hamid, Mr Hazzaa Al-Hasher, His Royal Highness
Prince Mohammed Bin Nawaf and the Royal Embassy of
Saudi Arabia, Dr Zamil Abu Zinada and the Ministry of
Communications in Jiddah, Nizar Abu Zinada, Abdul
Rahman Al Turkestani, Hanan Awad, Mr Khaldoon
Alsaadan, Manarat Jiddah School, Sami Nawar, Iyad
Mourad in Riyadh, and Ahmed, the best driver in Jiddah.

British Library Cataloguing in Publication Data
Senker, Cath
   Letters from Saudi Arabia. – (Letters from around
   the world)
   1. Saudi Arabia – Social life and customs – 21st century
– Juvenile literature
   I. Title
   953.8'053

ISBN-13: 9781842343814

Cover: Abdulatef (right) and his sister Ragad on the
terrace of their grandfather's house in Jiddah.
Title page: Abdulatef, Abdulrahman, Ragad and friends in
front of a mosque on the Corniche, the seafront in Jiddah.
This page: The capital city of Riyadh, showing the
Al-Faisaliah Tower in the centre.
Contents page: Abdulatef wears traditional Arab clothes
at school and for special occasions, but out of school he
wears Western-style clothing.
Glossary: Abdulatef serves coffee to guests dressed
in traditional Arab clothing.
Further Information page: A well-known woman journalist
talking on the Saudi national radio station.
Index: Arabic words projected on to the Jiddah Fountain,
one of the tallest fountains in the world.

Contents

My Country

Wednesday, 12 June

Alandalus Road 23
Jiddah 5759
Kingdom of Saudi Arabia

Dear Pat,

Marhaba! (That's Arabic for 'Hello'.)

My name is Abdulatef (say 'Abdula-teef') Anbar. I'm 10 years old and I live in Jiddah, a big city in Saudi Arabia. My full name is Abdulatef Jameel Ahmed Hassan Anbar. (Jameel is my dad's name, and Ahmed and Hassan are my grandfathers' names.) I've got one sister, Ragad, who's 9 and one brother, Abdulrahman, who's 8. Many families in Saudi Arabia have at least six children, so ours is quite small.

It's great to practise my English with a real English person. Write soon!

From

Abdulatef →

Here I am next to my dad, with Ragad and Abdulrahman, outside my grandfather's house.

The Kingdom of Saudi Arabia was formed in 1932. Most of the people are Arabs. There are also many foreign workers in the country. They are mainly from India, Bangladesh, the Philippines, Pakistan and Indonesia.

Saudi Arabia's place in the world.

Saudi Arabia covers four-fifths of the Arabian Peninsula. It is about the size of the whole of Western Europe.

Here is the old town of Jiddah. The traditional apartment blocks have wooden shutters to keep them cool. In the distance, you can see modern office blocks.

Jiddah is a modern city on the Red Sea. It has a large port where big ships enter and leave. The city also has many industries, including refining oil (making oil pure), and making steel, cement, clothing and pottery.

Jiddah has a modern road system and most people travel by car. Women are not allowed to drive, so they take taxis, travel with relatives, or use their own driver.

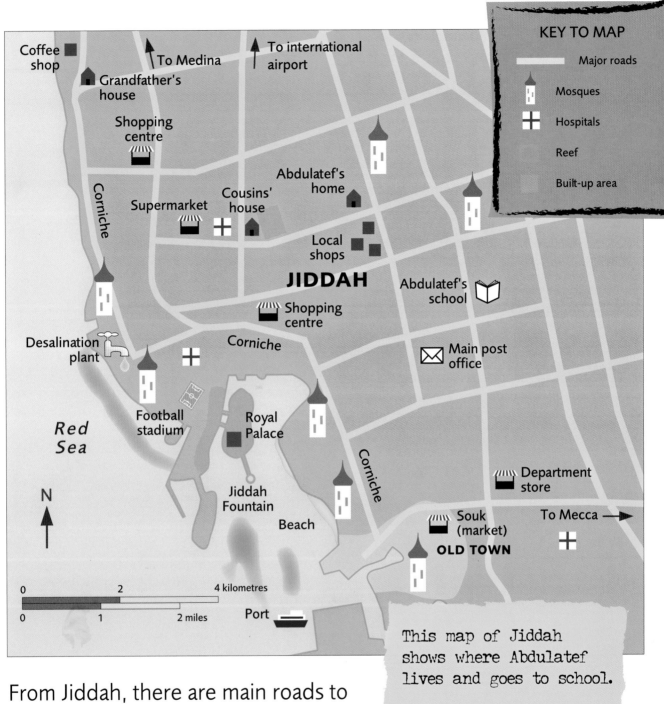

KEY TO MAP

Major roads

Mosques

Hospitals

Reef

Built-up area

Coffee shop

Grandfather's house

Shopping centre

To Medina

To international airport

Corniche

Supermarket

Cousins' house

Abdulatef's home

Local shops

JIDDAH

Abdulatef's school

Shopping centre

Corniche

Main post office

Desalination plant

Football stadium

Red Sea

Royal Palace

N

Jiddah Fountain

Beach

Corniche

Department store

Souk (market)

OLD TOWN

To Mecca →

0   2   4 kilometres

0   1   2 miles

Port

This map of Jiddah shows where Abdulatef lives and goes to school.

From Jiddah, there are main roads to the cities of Mecca and Medina. These are the holiest of Muslim cities. There is an international airport 35 kilometres away from the city. Every year, millions of Muslims fly into Jiddah to make their pilgrimage to Mecca and Medina.

Landscape and Weather

About a third of Saudi Arabia is desert. The Rub al-Khali (Empty Quarter), in the south, is the largest sand desert in the world. In the east, near Oman, there are salt flats. Along the Red Sea coast there are mountains.

Camels are desert animals that can go for up to ten months without drinking. This camel trader is taking his camels to a market.

Most of Saudi Arabia has a desert climate. In the summer, it is very hot and even in winter, it is still warm. There is very little rainfall, so drinking water has to be made from seawater, in a process called desalination. There are no permanent rivers, so farmers have to irrigate their crops.

This is a wadi, the bed of a river that is usually dry. After rain, plants can grow.

Jiddah's Climate

January	July
Temperature	Temperature
23°C	31°C
5mm	0mm
Rainfall	Rainfall

At Home

Like most people in Saudi Arabia, Abdulatef and his family live in a modern flat. They live on the first floor of the building. There are two other flats on the same floor.

Here is Abdulatef, standing outside his block of flats. There are three shops on the ground floor.

Abdulatef does his homework at the dining room table. Sometimes he looks things up on the Internet in English.

Abdulatef's home has a large living room, with a dining room, a kitchen, a bathroom and four bedrooms. There is an air-conditioning unit in each room to keep the flat cool. The windows are kept closed and covered to keep out the sun and the heat.

Like the rest of the flat, the living room has a cool, tiled floor with a rug on top. There are air-conditioning units either side of the TV.

Abdulatef shares this bedroom with his brother, but Ragad often joins them to play computer games and watch TV.

Many Saudi homes are divided into separate areas for males and females. Abdulatef's family shares the living areas, but it is only his mum and the family's maid who use the kitchen.

Muslims pray five times every day. Abdulatef says his prayers in the living room, with his prayer mat facing towards the holy city of Mecca.

Saturday, 19 July

Alandalus Road 23
Jiddah 5759
Kingdom of Saudi Arabia

Dear Pat,

I did a special ceremony today. I served Arabic *qahwa* (coffee) to our guests at home. We grind our coffee with a spice called cardamom to give it a spicy flavour. Then we boil the coffee for about half an hour. Our guests eat fresh dates or figs while they wait. Then we serve the coffee in little cups without handles. We half-fill each cup and serve more when it is empty. When people have had enough, they cover their cup with their hand and shake it from side to side.

Do you have any special ceremonies?

From

Abdulatef

Here I am, wearing traditional Arab clothes for the coffee ceremony. There are figs on the table.

Food and Mealtimes

For breakfast, Abdulatef has a dish called *shakshouka* (say 'shak-shooka'). Sometimes he has *ful* (say 'fool'). *Ful* is a bean dip eaten with a flat bread, called *khobz* (say 'hoobz').

This popular Saudi breakfast dish is called *shakshouka*. It is made from eggs and tomatoes.

For lunch and dinner, he eats traditional Arab dishes, such as kebabs with soup and vegetables. Another favourite is *kofta*, balls of minced beef or lamb with onions and spices. Abdulatef never eats ham, bacon or pork because Muslims are not allowed to.

Sometimes Abdulatef goes to a large supermarket with his father. He likes choosing from the display of cakes. The maid does most of the food shopping for the family.

Abdulatef's mother and the maid have prepared chicken soup, *tabbouleh* (cracked wheat with parsley), hummus, samosas and stuffed vine leaves.

At mealtimes, Abdulatef and his family help themselves from dishes in the middle of the table. They put food on their plate and eat it with their right hand or with cutlery. In many Saudi households, males and females eat separately, but Abdulatef's family eats together.

In Saudi Arabia, people drink lots of coffee and tea. Strong tea with plenty of sugar and fresh mint is popular. There is also an apricot drink made from dried apricots that have been pressed into thin sheets. The sheets are chopped and mixed with water to make a thick, tasty purée.

Thursday, 13 August

Alandalus Road 23
Jiddah 5759
Kingdom of Saudi Arabia

Dear Pat,

You asked what we eat and drink. Well, one of my favourite dishes is *mashkul* — fish filled with onion and spices. The fish is fried in oil and served with fresh limes on a bed of rice. Delicious!

Here's how you make a popular Arab drink, *shay bi naana* (mint tea). You will need: 4 teaspoons loose-leaf tea (or 4 tea bags); a handful of fresh mint, washed and drained (or dried mint); 4 teaspoons of sugar (or less if you prefer).

1. Put the tea and sugar in a warm teapot.
2. Boil 6 cups of water and add to the pot. Stir and allow to settle.
3. Add the mint and stir.
4. Allow to brew for 5 minutes.
5. Pour into small glasses. Serves 6–8.

Enjoy with cakes!

From

Abdulatef

Here's the tea that Ragad and our cousin Waad made.

School Day

Abdulatef is driven to school by his dad or the family's driver. School days in Saudi Arabia are from Saturday to Wednesday. They start and finish early to avoid the heat. Each day is from 7.30 a.m. to 1.30 p.m., with a half-hour break at 9.45 a.m.

Abdulatef started primary school when he was 6. He will stay there until he is 12. Then he will go to intermediate school for three years. When he is 15, he will go to secondary school for three years.

Here is Abdulatef and his friends outside his school. The school's name is written in Arabic above the door. It is Manarat Jiddah Elementary School.

There is a morning assembly most days. It is held at prayer time, so the children can pray together. The boys wear a traditional Arab *dishdasha* as their uniform.

There are two school terms, from September to early January and from February to May. Then there is a long summer holiday because of the hot weather. Schools have one week off at the time of the pilgrimage to Mecca. They have ten days' holiday for the festivals of Id ul-Fitr and Id ul-Adha.

At the back of Abdulatef's classroom, there is a picture of King Abdullah, the king of Saudi Arabia.

The school has a large computer room that the students use at least once a week.

Abdulatef learns Arabic, science, maths, Islam, history, geography and English. Girls and boys do not study together in Saudi Arabia. In Abdulatef's school, there are separate sections for girls and boys. They study mostly the same subjects, but girls do not do sport. They learn cooking and other skills that are useful in the home.

At school pick-up time, most children have their own family driver. Many are foreign workers from Indonesia. The cars cause a big traffic jam outside the school.

Thursday, 18 September

Alandalus Road 23
Jiddah 5759
Kingdom of Saudi Arabia

Dear Pat,

You asked about my school. My favourite subject is history. I love reading about the life of the Prophet Muhammad.

I'm also really into sport. At school we play basketball and swim in the outdoor pool. I go to football club every Wednesday evening. We play in the evening because it's too hot to play earlier in the day. It was funny to read about your weather. Rain never stops us playing because it only ever rains about once a year!

Maa salama! (Goodbye!)

From

Abdulatef

Here I am at my Wednesday-evening football club. There's a model of the Qur'an at the end of the pitch.

Off to Work

Abdulatef's father works at the national radio station in Jiddah. He works normal office hours. These are 8.30 a.m. to 2 p.m. and 4.30 to 7 p.m., Saturday to Wednesday.

Most Saudi women do not work outside the home. But Abdulatef's mother teaches English to kindergarten children (four- and five-year-olds) in the girls' section of his school.

Abdulatef's dad (left) talks with a workmate about the radio programmes they are planning.

Saudi Arabia has the largest oil supply in the world. The country depends on the sale of oil. Other important industries include making chemicals and plastics. About a quarter of workers have jobs in industry, while about 60 per cent work in services such as communications. Most foreign workers have jobs in the oil industry or services.

There are still traditional types of work in Saudi Arabia. These men are fishing on Jiddah's seafront.

This is the oil refinery in Jiddah, where oil is made pure to make useful products such as petrol and diesel fuel.

Free Time

In their free time, Saudis enjoy visiting relatives and eating together. There are no bars, cinemas or theatres in Saudi Arabia. Instead, men like to meet in coffee shops to chat, play games and drink coffee. Women see their friends in each other's homes.

Abdulatef likes taking camel rides along Jiddah's seafront. Here, his friend Tharal takes a turn.

In this coffee shop in a large tent, men play computer games and drink coffee.

Like many Saudis, Abdulatef enjoys playing and watching football and basketball. He supports local Saudi teams. Arsenal is his favourite international football team.

Abdulatef's dad has 30 days' holiday, as well as the religious holidays, each year. His mum has all the school holidays. Most years, the family flies to Egypt or Syria for their holidays to visit relatives. Many Saudis have relatives in other Arab countries.

Abdulatef's cousins often come to his house to play. Here, they are playing a word game that always makes them laugh.

Religion and Festivals

Islam began in Saudi Arabia and it is the religion of all Saudis. Every year, about 2 million Muslims from around the world make their pilgrimage to the holy cities of Mecca and Medina.

Islam is a way of life. In public, everyone wears long clothes to cover their body. In all schools and workplaces, people stop what they are doing to pray five times a day. On Fridays, men and boys attend the mosque, while women and girls say their prayers at home.

Abdulatef reads from the Qur'an every day at home. He goes to the mosque with his father on Fridays.

Abdulatef prays five times a day, getting up early for the first prayers. Here, he is praying with his whole school.

Friday, 3 October

Alandalus Road 23
Jiddah 5759
Kingdom of Saudi Arabia

Dear Pat,

Did I tell you about Ramadan? It takes place every year and lasts for a month. During the whole month, adults fast (don't eat or drink) from dawn to sunset. Children don't have to fast, but I've fasted since I was nine. It's not too hard. It's tiring because we go to bed late and get up before dawn to eat breakfast. But it's a very special time when we think about our beliefs as Muslims.

At the end of Ramadan, it's the festival of Id ul-Fitr. There's no school for a week. We dress in new clothes and get together with friends and family to eat huge feasts. Everyone wishes each other 'Id Mubarak' – 'Happy Id'.

What special days do you celebrate?

From

Abdulatef

We break the fast by first eating a few dates. Then we have a huge meal.

Fact File

Main industries: Oil production, refining petrol, petrochemicals, other chemicals, cement, construction, plastics, ship and aircraft repair.

Currency: Saudi riyal, divided into hallalahs (1 riyal=100 hallalahs).

Capital city: Riyadh is the capital of Saudi Arabia. It is in the middle of the country.

Other major cities: Jiddah, Mecca, Medina and Ad-Dammam.

Population: 27 million, including 5.6 million foreigners who are working in Saudi Arabia.

Size: 1,960, 582km^2

Language: Arabic

Religion: Islam is the religion of Saudi Arabia. Foreign workers of other faiths are not allowed to practise their religions.

Famous buildings: The best-known buildings are in the two holy cities of Mecca and Medina. The holiest place in Islam is a cube-shaped building called the Kaaba, in Mecca. Muslims believe that it is the oldest holy building. All Muslims worldwide face towards the Kaaba when they pray. It is surrounded by the Sacred Mosque. The second holiest building is the Prophet's Mosque in Medina, the first Muslim city.

Flag: Green, a traditional colour for Islamic flags, with the Islamic statement of faith in God written in Arabic. A sword below the writing stands for justice, and for the first Saudi king, Abd al-Aziz al-Saud.

Largest desert: The Rub' al-Khali (Empty Quarter) covers an area of about 650,000km^2 and has many sand dunes. It is mainly in south-eastern Saudi Arabia, but it is also in Yemen, Oman and the United Arab Emirates.

Famous people: The Prophet Muhammad, who brought the message of the religion of Islam, came from what is now Saudi Arabia. In the early twentieth century, Ibn Saud conquered the area that makes up the modern country. He became its first king, King Abd al-Aziz al-Saud, in 1932. Many people worldwide see the Saudi, Osama Bin Laden, as the leader of the radical Islamic group Al-Qaeda.

Highest mountain: Mount Sawda' (3,133m), in the south-west of the country, near the city of Abha.

Stamps: Stamps in Saudi Arabia show members of the royal family, transport, the oil industry, holy places and sport.

29

Glossary

Arabic One of several similar languages spoken in Saudi Arabia, Egypt, Iraq, Lebanon, Jordan, Syria and North Africa.

desalination A process where salt is removed from seawater.

dunes Hills of sand in the desert, formed by the wind.

flat bread A thin, flat Arab bread, like pitta bread.

harbour An area of water protected from the open sea by strong walls, where ships can shelter.

Id ul-Adha The festival when Muslims remember how Abraham offered to kill his son to obey God.

Id ul-Fitr The festival at the end of Ramadan. Everyone wears new clothes and eats a special meal. Children are given sweets and presents.

irrigate To supply water to crops through pipes or tunnels.

Mecca A city in western Saudi Arabia. It is the holiest of Muslim cities.

pilgrimage A journey to a holy place for religious reasons.

port A place where ships load and unload goods.

Prophet Muhammad The founder of the religion of Islam, who lived in Arabia.

Ramadan The Muslim month during which adult Muslims fast (do not eat or drink) during daylight hours.

refinery A factory where a substance such as oil is made pure.

salt flats Flat areas covered in salt, where water has evaporated, leaving behind salt.

wadi The bed of a river or stream that is usually dry except at rare times when it rains. Then plants can grow in it.

Further Information

Information books:

Children's Encyclopaedia of Arabia by Mary Beardwood (Stacey International, 2006)

Countries in the News: Saudi Arabia by Cath Senker (Franklin Watts, 2006)

Saudi Arabia: A Question and Answer Book by Kathleen W Deady (Capstone Press, 2005)

Saudi Arabia: A True Book by Wende Fazion (Scholastic, 1999)

A Ticket to Saudi Arabia by Laurie Halse Anderson (Carolrhoda, 2001)

Fiction:

A is for Arabia by Julia Johnson (Stacey International, 2003)

Saluki, Hound of the Bedouin by Julia Johnson (Stacey International, 2005)

Websites:

Child Fun
www.childfun.com/modules.php?
name=News&file=article&sid=184
Activities and recipes on the theme of Saudi Arabia.

Explore Saudi Arabia
www.exploresaudiarabia.com
Facts about the country and young people's lives there.

If your school would like to make contact with a school in Saudi Arabia, go to:
www.exploresaudiarabia.com/today/school_project.htm

Islam for Children
http://atschool.eduweb.co.uk/carolrb/islam/islamintro.html
Includes history of Islam, daily life, mosques and festivals.

The World Factbook
www.cia.gov/cia/publications/factbook/index.html
Facts and figures about Saudi Arabia and other countries.

Index